DAYBREAK
DAILY MESSAGES TO ILLUMINATE
YOUR SPIRITUAL LIFE

DAYBREAK

Daily Messages to Illuminate
Your Spiritual Life

SUSAN DAWN

PENNSYLVANIA

Susan Dawn Spiritual Connections, LLC
Lititz, PA
www.susandawnspiritual.com

Library of Congress Control Number: 2023908630
ISBN Paperback: 979-8-9882881-0-7
ISBN Digital: 979-8-9882881-2-1

Cover Design by Andrew Brown, designforwriters.com
Interior Design by Rebecca Brown, designforwriters.com

Visit the author's website at www.susandawnspiritual.com

Printed in the United States of America

FOR ANYONE TRYING TO FIND
THEIR LIGHT IN THE DARK

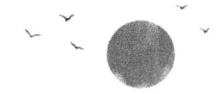

INTRODUCTION

INHALE LOVE. EXHALE FEAR. REPEAT.

IT SEEMS SO SIMPLE, DOESN'T it? Love more. Fear less. It's such a straightforward concept until it becomes complicated. It's an easy practice until we actually put it into practice. This is the paradox of living a spiritual life within a human existence—simple truths twist themselves until they become complex, and we get a little bit lost, a little bit disconnected, and a little bit off-track.

All my life, I've felt the Universe guiding me, yet it was my own stubborn humanness that kept me from fully trusting where I was being led. Through a keen sense of self-awareness and natural sensitivity, I learned early on to follow my intuition in navigating difficult life events, nurturing the spark of creative adventures, or opening up to surprising soul connections. But trusting my own intuition felt different from trusting the Universe. I didn't yet know that they were one in the same.

My deep desire to understand myself began in the pages of my earliest diary and would translate to a personal blog years later, where I would then spend over a decade attempting to figure out who I am and why I'm here and why the world is the way it is (and how to change it for the better). That journey of discovery didn't seem to have a place in Sunday services, where I was encouraged to follow others' truths rather than exploring my own. I felt disconnected from myself and from God, more confused by faith than calmed by it. I always felt there was something more, something that religion itself couldn't provide. It seemed we were a part of an infinite puzzle, its pieces scattered throughout the Universe, and religion held only one piece of it. I wanted the rest of the puzzle. I wanted the big picture. I wanted to know more.

Something was waking up inside of me even at that young age—a spark of truth igniting in my soul, though I didn't have a name for it. I wanted a name for it. I wanted to know myself, to figure out where I belonged. And so, I began to research other faiths, hoping that one of them would speak to me, that I would have that "a-ha!" moment and the rest of the puzzle would fall into place. The problem was that all of them spoke to me.

Instead of belonging somewhere, I felt like I belonged everywhere.

The more I explored, the more I realized that my beliefs weren't founded in religion. At least, not in any one religion, and certainly not one I could name. The fundamentals of what I believed, however—what felt true beyond my cognitive understanding—crossed those boundaries. Life stems from a source, and that source is Love.

When I was in my early years of high school, I read a quote from Thomas Paine's *Rights of Man* in which it was summed up: "My country is the world and my religion is to do good." Those words resonated with me like nothing else.

Simple. Honest. Maybe it really wasn't as complicated as we made it seem.

It made more sense than anything else I'd read or studied. Religion was too confining for me, too structured. There were too many unanswered questions, and I couldn't accept that faith meant being led blindly when we have the capability of seeing for ourselves.

Faith, I began to understand, was about trusting your own truth.

So I began the journey of discovering what my truth was...

Catalyst events of multiple losses, chronic illness, and meeting soul connections plunged me deeper than ever into the core of myself and my connection with God. Of course, I went kicking and screaming. My human self, so scarred by past experiences, didn't know how to let go and surrender, and though it all seemed so easy and simple when I was younger, those experiences had created a feeling of betrayal wherein I lost my faith and lost myself. I felt fragmented, abandoned by the Universe that I had once been so connected to. My anger at God for this suffering created a separation within myself. Why would a benevolent God desert us in our time of greatest need? How could faith be asked of us when there was so much pain in the world? What was faith, anyway?

Slowly, as I began to heal my health, I also began to heal my spirit. I began to understand that it wasn't pain God was bringing into my life through these experiences, but love. Strength. Courage. It was everything I would need to walk through the illusion of who I thought I was in order to come home to myself.

In 2017, when I was activated to the next-level of my spiritual journey, I was initiated into a process of full surrender—opening my mind, expanding my heart, and placing my full trust in the Universe to guide me on my soul's path. The more I began to open up to parts of myself I had forgotten or suppressed, the more at home I felt. I was connecting to God again.

I began my YouTube channel, *Susan Dawn Spiritual Connections*, a year later after hearing the call from the Universe. Of course, I resisted at first. I didn't know what I was doing or why I was being guided in this new direction—and have I mentioned yet how stubborn I can be? But I knew from past experiences what it meant to trust that soul-nudge, and over the months that followed, I began to explore where I was being led as I deepened my connection to myself and to God. My YouTube channel became the story of my own spiritual evolution as much as it grew into a community of support and empowerment for others along their personal paths.

Daybreak is the culmination of writings from my own soul-growth journey as well as six years of channeling collective messages and Daily Energy Draws on my YouTube channel, compiled into a digestible format as guidance and motivation for your spiritual life. Use this book as *you* feel called to! Read the book cover-to-cover, begin your day with a morning message, or trust your intuition to guide you to a random message to inspire you when you need it most. These messages are prompts meant for conscious reflection within the context of your own soul's truth. Use your intuition to discern how they relate to you as guidance to inspire and illuminate your life.

When you're in the midst of a spiritual awakening, it's hard to see the light within the darkness; it's hard to see the forest for the trees. But it's here that we become, finding the strength, the courage, and the faith to reveal both our humanity and our spiritual truth. It's here that we grow, giving space and respect to the shadowed corners of ourselves while acknowledging the light itself.

It's here that we rise, remembering that day always follows the night.

With love,
Susan

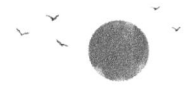

Gather up your courage, light the fire within you, and face the darkness with a warrior heart. Once the sun rises, you'll be transformed into something greater than you can even imagine.

Never forget that you're meant to be here as part of the world. You're here for a reason that you orchestrated with your spirit team for the beautiful expression of your soul's evolution that the Universe then experiences through you. Allow yourself to rise into your full divinity. Step up and become all of who you are.

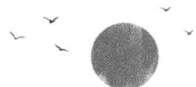

Begin today by expressing gratitude. What can you be grateful for in your life right now, in this moment? What are your present experiences showing you? Look for the blessings, and you'll understand the lessons.

Your soul is naturally expansive and creative, wanting to give you the life experience of your dreams, including healthy and loving relationships, stability and abundance in your physical world, and opportunities for wish fulfillment. Where you may have once been in resistance to these changes due to old beliefs and mindsets of scarcity and lack, you're choosing to follow the path you're guided towards, which is paving its way to a beautiful new creation.

Trust that all is working out for your best and highest good as you're orchestrating with GodSource as the powerful co-creator that you are. Release the resistance and recognize your inner strength. All is well.

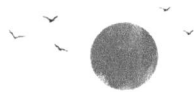

Your emotions are your navigational blueprint for peace and balance. When you're being triggered, it's to guide you back to more love and compassion within yourself. Where are you finding yourself being triggered? What feels out of alignment? Find your place of peace within.

Return to the innocent child you were and allow yourself to have fun, explore, and play! Play is a proponent of love, which is the key to understanding the expansive nature of your own creative being. Tend to the childlike wonder that resides within you.

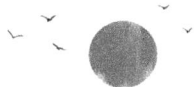

You've come to this planet to share in the universal experience of love. You're being called to rise now and remember that your soul is one with the very fabric of creation. No separation exists within the Universe. Rise in the light of who you are and share your love with the world around you.

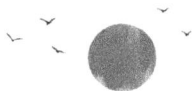

If you want it, you must trust it. If you feel it, you must have faith in it. What you want will always be provided. What is meant for you will always make its way towards you. No matter the challenges, you are your only obstacle.

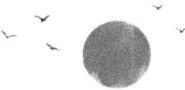

You're letting fear hold you back in some area of your life—fear of change, fear of love, fear of the unknown. Remember that when you're in an energy of fear, you're blocking love which is who you naturally are. Let love flow and watch how you rise.

How strong is your faith? Remove doubt by surrendering your fears and concerns to the Universe, trusting that it always has your best and highest good in mind. Know that everything is unfolding exactly as it's meant to and let the Universe surprise you in magical ways.

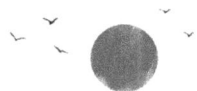

You're building a firm foundation and planting roots in your own life through creating a greater sense of harmony within yourself and in relationship with the world around you. You're stepping back into your power, your confidence, and your worth by recognizing the divine being that you are, which is making room for future abundance, love, and prosperity. The fear of being constantly uprooted is in the past, and now you're anchored into an energy of harmony, peace, and love. Well done!

Release expectations for how you think something should be and step into a place of receiving and allowing. This energy of surrender is what brings you into alignment with the Universe. Feel the release of resistance and fill up with the energy of joy and play.

The Universe is a playful energy that wants to support and surprise you. When you're in a place of pleasant surprise and joy at what life is offering you, it raises your vibrations so the Universe can bring you more of the same. Be present in the here and now and release control and the need to know.

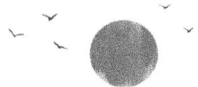

If you're feeling out of harmony or in a state of conflict, ground yourself to the Earth through remembering your oneness with the divine energy of all that is.

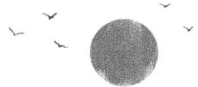

Why are you holding yourself back from stepping into the unknown? Can you have faith that there's something better ahead than what you're leaving behind? When you step out of your comfort zone, you may have no idea what's in store for you, but this, too, can be a blessing. You're on the precipice, at the edge of something new. Do you trust with full faith? Now take that leap.

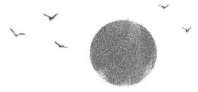

Focus on the journey, not the destination. Your dreams, wishes, and goals are coming to fruition, so release expectations and settle into appreciating the journey, as you're well on your way to bringing your manifestations to light.

Everything you experience is a stepping stone for your creation. Trust and have faith that your dreams, wishes, and goals are manifesting as part of your evolution. Release your limiting beliefs around timing, and trust in the divine order of the Universe to bring you more than you ever thought possible.

Step into the joy of life! Call in your abundance and align with your manifestations through feelings of joy and bliss. Leave the past behind you and step into the sunshine of this new phase of your life!

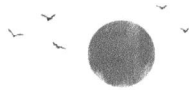

What seem like miracles are just your own creations coming to life in the physical realm. You are more powerful in your own divinity than you can even imagine. What are you creating?

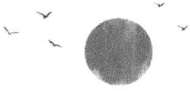

The path is yours to walk. Focus on embodying your highest self and living your authentic truth. You know the purity of your own heart, the strength of your own soul. Don't let anyone try to silence you. Don't let anyone try to dim your light.

You are divinely protected as you call back parts of yourself that you once gave away to others through power, control, and sacrifice. As you continue your soul growth journey, you're taking charge of your life and learning to speak your truth. Reclaim these aspects of yourself.

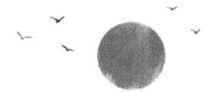

You are not alone. The entirety of the spirit realm is behind you, not just supporting you, but honoring your growth and evolution. It takes courage to come to Earth in this time and space, and you were a brave soul who made that choice because you have the resilience, wisdom, and strength to overcome this planet's challenges. Continue to heal your own karma and shine your light as a beacon for others. Your ancestors and spirit team are so grateful for the work you're doing. Keep going!

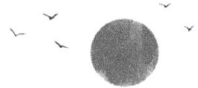

Your spirit team is with you, always guiding and supporting you. Trust in them as you trust in yourself.

Something new is being created within your life, particularly when it comes to partnership. How are you collaborating with others? How are you feeling inspired in your life and harnessing your sacred creative energy for the metamorphosis of your own soul's journey? Go within and reflect on how and what you're co-creating with others so you can bring it fully to fruition.

Your intuitive gifts are opening, and you're stepping more into your soul's purpose. Your passions are naturally a part of this. Follow that passion into greater purpose. Allow the two to align.

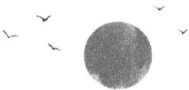

Don't be afraid to express your gifts. Shine your light and step into who you truly are by speaking your truth and sharing your love. You begin your true soul mission of helping to shift the planet to one of balance, harmony, and love through this expression of yourself.

You've been in a cocoon of healing wherein you've been deeply connecting to your emotional body—perhaps for the first time or after significant suppression. Life might feel stagnant or void-like, but have patience with yourself and your inner journey as you continue to heal. A new start is coming as you keep releasing the rising emotions that have held you back in the past. You'll only remain stagnant if you continue in the resistance of your personal truth. Trust the path you're on.

The cocoon is breaking open, and you're beginning to emerge as your Higher Self. Where it was once painful to let go of all you thought you were, all you thought you had, or all you thought you needed to be, now you're recognizing all you truly are and always have been: this is who you are within the embodiment of your own sacredness. The fruits of your transformation are taking shape as you're finding your footing and planting new roots through the wisdom you've gained along the way.

Awakening means stripping away the masks, the false beliefs, and the parts of yourself that were only an illusion. It's about waking up to the soul of who you are...and who you aren't. Who are you? You are love.

It's time to remember the truth of who you are. It's time to remember that you are limitless, and what you imagine doesn't begin to touch what is truly possible.

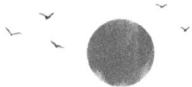

The Universe is bringing you your wish fulfillment, but you have to meet it halfway. Don't be afraid to be bold and take action. By opening up your heart instead of blocking your blessings, you're telling the Universe that you trust in your co-creatorship. Take that leap of faith. The Universe will always have your back.

You are the creator of your own destiny, manifesting your life and your abundance. Don't ever negate your own power. You get to choose which story you write. How will you create your destiny?

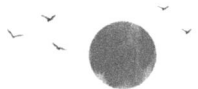

The Universe is a magical place. Very soon you're going to see the physical manifestations of the intentions you had set and the growth you have done. Work with the Universe to take action for your heart's deepest desires and then allow the magic of your manifestation to unfold.

You're in the process of overcoming and releasing something that is no longer serving you, including toxic relationships, situations, and beliefs. The door is opening and peace is settling into your life. Trust that you have the strength to move through this cycle. If you're feeling overwhelmed, connect with those who support your growth.

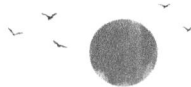

It's safe for you to embrace love in your life. It's safe for you to open up your heart and be vulnerable with another for the simple fact that you've manifested this through your own self-love. You've reached a place in your journey where you have shifted your energy, and now you have attracted the person your heart is calling for who will be in alignment with you. Listen to what your heart is saying.

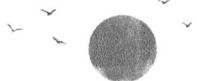

Love is the language of the Universe. You may have forgotten the words temporarily, but look inside yourself. Your soul is tuned to the song of love.

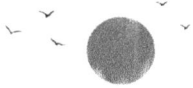

Forgiveness is a major part of the healing journey. You cannot come back to love without forgiveness. You cannot fully open up your heart if you don't hold forgiveness within its vessel. Where do you need to forgive yourself or others?

You're breaking the chains of the past, letting go of your own self-imprisonment, and opening up to more love so that you have more love to share. Grant yourself the space and compassion for this healing to take place.

A difficult cycle is coming to an end. Your spirit team wants you to know how proud they are of you for how you've overcome and transformed amidst the challenges of your journey. Here you are, remembering that you are not the experiences, the beliefs, or the stories. You are love itself.

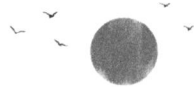

No matter how difficult or precarious the path might seem, the Universe is guiding you on your spiritual journey. Leave the baggage of the past behind because it's no longer needed. You're at a stage in your evolution where you've closed out those old cycles, and now it's time for you to level up.

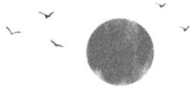

Are you willing to level up in your own evolution? Are you ready to step forward and be a guiding light for others? Trust that the Universe is guiding you just the same. Go forward fearlessly in the embodiment of love, for that love shines the light for others to see.

Don't let your light dim. You don't know who's facing their shadows. Don't let your flame go out. You don't know who's feeling its warmth.

If you knew the amount of love and support you have surrounding you, you would never feel lost, helpless, or confused. Your spirit team is here to help you navigate this difficult terrain called life. Call on them for guidance, love, and support through your meditations and prayers anytime you find yourself in need.

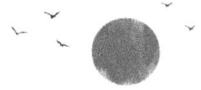

When the heart is blocked, there isn't a steady flow of love, creating imbalance within connections with others and yourself. This block is simply fear, but there's no reason to fear your connection with another. Now it's time to enjoy the love that exists between you by bringing more harmony to the connection. Believe that it's safe for you to love and open your heart to receive.

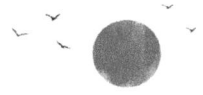

Look to where your energy has to shift and your patterns around communication have to change to bring more harmony into your connections and your life. Communication is the bridge that brings you together.

It takes being truly honest with yourself—diving deep within and uncovering the truth of how you feel in the present moment—for the old layer of false protection to be shed and your heart to be revealed. In that moment of raw vulnerability, you change the course of your life. It's in this awareness and acknowledgement of your shadow that you realize the power you have to harness the light. Keep shining.

Show the world your real, your raw, your vulnerable. Show the world your kindness and compassion. Show the world how you follow your heart and lead from your soul. Show the world your humanity, for it's here you are divine.

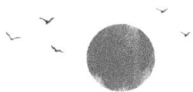

You're on this journey because you wanted to remember your divinity—that you are soul, love, and part of the Universe itself. Rather than focusing on the external world that creates illusions to the contrary, you're remembering that everything is created within you. What is it that you want to create? What is it that you dream of? Nothing is impossible.

Everything comes in its perfect, divine timing for your soul's growth established by you before your incarnation at the onset of Time itself. Trust in this and trust in yourself. There are no mistakes.

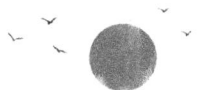

You're having a human experience because this helps you to understand the depth of love that you are. When you're avoiding the human aspect of yourself to focus on your spiritual nature, you're denying a critical part of your very being and creating dualistic thinking when the human aspect and the soul are meant to be unified. Your human experience is an expression of the totality of you. Embrace all that you are.

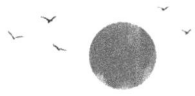

It's time to focus on your physical world. Where have you been neglecting your responsibilities? Where have you been avoiding yourself? Take stock of your life and put more effort into the places in need of nurturing so all can come back into balance.

Everyone in this world is a teacher if you have a willingness to learn. From strangers to neighbors to animals to your beloved, there exists, within the soul connection, an energy of pure, unconditional love, forgiveness, and support for your growth. This is GodSource's love for you working through the world.

You're in need of support, and support is readily available to you. Call upon trusted friends, family, and community, and reach out to those who help you feel heard and understood. They are in your life for a divine purpose. Accept the help that's being offered as you connect with those who feed your soul.

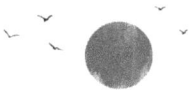

In times when you feel lost, know that you are guided. In times when you feel discouraged, know that you are supported. In times when you feel lonely, know that you are held.

If you've been doubting yourself or your journey, or if you're experiencing a crisis of faith, this is your sign to keep believing. You're being led even through the darkest nights. Take this time to sit in sanctuary with yourself. Quiet the mind and outside influences to connect more deeply to your soul's truth—the space within the heart that speaks in honor of itself. Revisit the building blocks of who you are or create a new foundation aligned with your soul. Let this experience draw you closer to your connection to yourself and your faith.

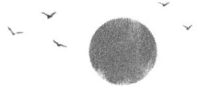

Through the darkness comes the light, and after destruction comes creation. If you've been experiencing struggle, challenges, or even a Dark Night of the Soul, know that the skies are clearing. You will come out the other side of this stronger, braver, and wiser.

This period of your life is teaching you about yourself, asking you to go within the pathways of your being and explore the deep-seated beliefs that hold you back in limitation and lack. Through these experiences, you understand not only what you're capable of—your strength, your courage, your tenacity, your resilience—but also your desires and dreams that have been locked away in the hidden corners of your heart. In the silence and stillness of yourself, you begin to heal those wounds that guarded your heart, letting love flow through and fill every inch with hope. Like a spring bursting forth to create an abundant oasis where there was once only desert, your life is expanding, or is about to expand, in beautiful ways due to the growth within.

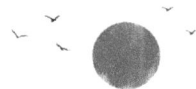

Who you are now in this stage of your evolution is different from who you used to be, which can fill you with uncertainty, much like a newborn opening their eyes for the first time or a toddler taking their first steps. This is part of the process. Look inside yourself and see how you've transformed and evolved. Do you really want to go back? Would you trade walking for crawling, waking for sleeping? Have patience with yourself. It takes a lot of energy to release who you thought you were in order to become who you truly are.

Self-awareness is the key to any growth. Refuse to look at yourself, and you stunt your own evolution. You have the courage to embark on this journey of self-discovery. Looking at the light within allows you to open up to self-love, but looking at the shadows is where the transformation really begins. Believe that you are brave enough.

Trust in yourself. No matter how others may discredit you, no matter how your experiences are invalidated, no matter how little support you feel you have… Trust in yourself. Keep your heart open, remain humble, and continue in alignment with your soul's truth.

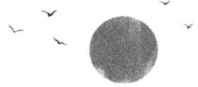

Continue to have faith and believe in the situation at hand, for the seeds you had long ago planted are beginning to poke through the soil and sprout their first bud. This has been a time of learning to trust your intuition, letting the call of your heart guide you through periods of uncertainty. Now that you've been opening up your heart to more faith, those manifestations are taking root in the physical plane. Your prayers are being heard.

Do you know how powerful a creator you are? Your thoughts not only become physical manifestations, but they create your entire reality around you. If you focus on the negative, you will always see the negative in situations and experiences. If you focus on the past, you'll only perpetuate old patterns and cycles. The Universe is blessing you with an opportunity to shift your perspective to more beauty, joy, and abundance. Start with even the smallest step, and begin to see a new reality reflected back to you.

You have the power to choose your reality, with that reality aligning to your best and highest potential for your soul's growth and evolution. Your current reality is simply the manifestations of a past version of you. In every moment, you're manifesting your future by the thoughts you think, the beliefs you hold, and the stories you tell yourself. Don't make yourself small to fit into the world that was. Keep shining your light to align to what can be.

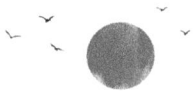

Speak your truth out loud—the one you've been holding onto, the one you've been fearful of admitting to yourself or the world. Feel that truth rise from the recesses of your heart and feel how good it is to set it free. This is your beginning.

Your power lies in your self-expression. It's your ability to take responsibility for your actions and your life. It's your awareness of the ego-self while connecting with your Higher Self through the integration of love and compassion. It's the choices you make in the highest frequency that move you from lack to limitlessness. Power is your inner authority and personal sovereignty and how you express this empowerment as a whole. Don't be afraid to express the fullness of who you are.

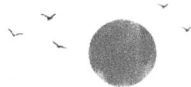

Your story is meant to serve as a guidepost for your life while sharing your story acts as a guidepost for others. Recognize the battles you've fought, who you've transformed into, and how you've become a stronger and more compassionate version of the person you once were. Own your story and claim this part of yourself.

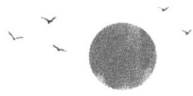

Who you were yesterday is not who you are today. Apologize to that past version of you. Find forgiveness in your heart for actions, thoughts, or beliefs that kept you from who you truly are and who you choose to be now. Say thank you for the lessons and the experiences that have helped you to grow. And then, love yourself. Say these powerful words out loud as you look in a mirror: "I love you. I forgive you." Repeat this until you feel it in your heart.

Forgive the past to let love in. By holding onto your past, you're blocking the flow of love into this present moment. What are you still holding onto that is no longer serving your highest good? Where are you blocking your love?

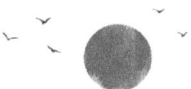

Be open to receiving the gift of love. You've been wishing for it and manifesting it, and now it's here, but are you still blocking it from fully entering your life? Embrace this opportunity for love by opening your heart and releasing expectations for how it comes to be. Allow this love to flow and grow.

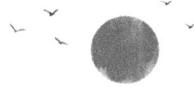

Love is not just one thing. Love is for yourself and others. It's how you give and how you receive. It's how you nurture yourself and the healthy habits you engage. Love is all. Love is everything. Love is you.

Loving yourself and loving others both have healing properties. To love others, you must fully love yourself. To love yourself is to love others. Open yourself up to expressing yourself within how and who you love.

Your inner child is calling to you… Sit with your inner child in your sacred space—either in your mind's eye or a physical place. Imagine yourself holding, comforting, and nurturing them in the way you long to be held, comforted, and nurtured. Tell your inner child you love them. Tell them about your transformation, your evolution, how proud you are of them and the person they've become. Love them dearly. Remind them they are safe.

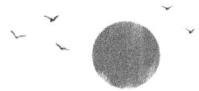

It's hard to leap into the unknown, but is it really unknown to your soul that charted your path before your emergence into this world? Is it unknown to your spirit team and ancestors who hold you in divine protection and limitless support? In every single moment, you're already moving forward… With the next heartbeat and the next and the next, your present is already becoming the past. So why fear the future when your power lies in the here and now? You have the choice in the present to create your next moment, which builds your entire future going forward. Every now moment is a moment of creation.

Place a hand upon your heart and calm your breath. Feel the love that embraces you, that surrounds you, that nourishes you. You are safe in this world. You are safe in this body. You are safe in this lifetime. Rest your weary head on the pillow of your faith and surrender your anxious mind.

Have you been burning yourself out? You've been pushing and pushing to make a change, and the forward momentum from the work you've done will be visible soon enough. Now is the time to rest and recharge so your light becomes bright once again. Have confidence in yourself and let your inner beacon shine forth as you continue forward. Trust that all truly is well and that everything is working out in your favor in perfect, divine timing.

Steady wins the race. Be practical and have a plan to make sure that whatever you're pursuing, building, or creating is done right. Rather than rushing ahead, take it step-by-step, allowing your intuition to lead from a grounded place. Once you get the momentum going, it will be full-steam ahead.

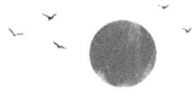

What would you do if you knew you were so divinely supported? What "risks" would you take? How would you open your heart? How deeply would you love? Begin to recognize that the only true risk is one in which there is no faith.

If you're looking too closely at a problem, you can't see the bigger picture. Pull back and make the conscious decision to see through a new lens, shifting your perspective to find another solution. It's here you'll be guided in your next steps.

There's a divine healing that's trying to make its way into your life right now. Your soul is calling for this growth and self-discovery, and your physical world deeply wishes to reflect this. The old cycle was created from an outdated version of yourself. Because of your transformation, you're ready to embark on the new. Trust your heart and intuition to help you navigate this healing. Keep releasing what wants to be let go and allow yourself to discover the expanded version of your life. Recommit to the highest version of yourself and embrace the wonder, beauty, and joy this creates.

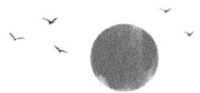

Keep exploring what lights you up. Let go of the path of struggle and survival and embrace your journey of playfulness and passion. That which excites you about life is what helps you embrace the gift of life, which builds the momentum for your creations.

You have everything you need within you. You have the ability to be materially and financially stable. You have the ability to be emotionally secure. You have the ability to be confident, joyful, and loved. You have the ability to be a master of yourself. You have this ability because this is what you already are. Remembering this truth is what your journey is all about.

You're moving closer and closer to reaching success by breaking through old habits and templates that might have kept you locked in doubt. Where there was once a lack of clarity, now you're seeing the way forward. Breakthroughs and revelations in the form of surprises or sudden upheavals may further push you to embrace your own divinity, which will continue to create forward momentum for your life.

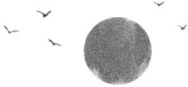

You're an alchemist burning away dense energy that binds you to lower thought forms, lifting yourself higher to become one with all. Don't forget your power.

Embrace the blossoming of this new you as you step forward into your new world. Call on your angels and guides for support if you're still feeling trepidation. Open your heart up to receive and allow them to fill you with strength so that you can feel confident in this next phase of your life. Don't be afraid to show the world who you are now as you're becoming more of who you were always meant to be.

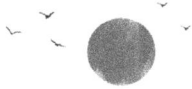

Speak up! Where do you need to tap into that eternal (internal) wisdom? Where do you need to be more expressive? Tune into who you are through self-awareness and self-expression.

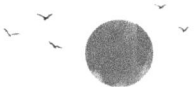

Being authentically you means expressing who you are on every level. How are you wielding that sword of truth for yourself and being true to who you are? How are you communicating that to others and receiving others' communication? Step more into this energy of finding the power within yourself and remember that truth and expression both hold power. Being authentically you means expressing who you are on every level.

Don't let pride get in the way, for pride only leads to resistance and chaos within the heart. Restore balance by allowing for a resolution of conflict. Those old endings make way for brand new, bright beginnings.

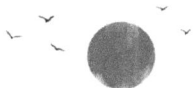

The only thing you'll ever need to do in this life is show up exactly as you are, with all of your light and all of your love. This is how you change the world.

Your journey might look like the great unknown, and you may fear that things aren't working out as you wish them to, but that's where the Universe is calling for you to have more faith and trust. When you let go of control, you release resistance. When you release resistance, you raise in vibration and frequency, which the Universe immediately responds to. Keep an open mind, let go of expectations, and love your journey as it unfolds.

New pathways are being cleared and illuminated. You might not be able to see everything at the moment, but know that your spirit team is aligning it all for you. Trust in them, for they are one with you.

You've been feeling a growing sense of newness in your energy field and an excitement for what's being created, though you may feel stuck and fear that nothing is changing in your physical world. Trust the process. You may still be releasing residual aspects of your past, but the more you hold onto those old fears, beliefs, or mindsets, the more you're creating stagnancy in your journey. Keep your focus turned towards the future you're aligning to while remaining present in a state of patient acceptance.

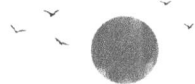

Be gentle with yourself. Don't force anything, but be in the energy of flow, trusting where your heart is leading. You're exactly when and where you're meant to be.

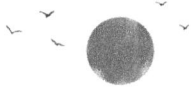

Trust the path of the soul and have faith in the divine guidance of the heart. Your enlightenment is your awareness of self. Through your awareness, you are able to shift patterns, change outdated beliefs, heal pain, rewrite social conditioning and programming, and ultimately reclaim your sovereignty. Your profound acceptance of yourself within your own authority is what moves mountains both in your personal life and in the world.

The Universe is supporting you. Not only are you co-creating with the Universe, you are an aspect of the Universe, which is constantly responding to your vibrational alignment. Where are you feeling out of alignment with yourself? Where is your life not reflective of the life you want to lead? Manifestation starts with you, so if you're feeling stuck, low, or in a negative thought pattern, have fun, create, dance, and play to raise your vibrations and manifest the life you dream.

Gratitude begets more reasons for gratitude. Create a gratitude practice to help you recognize the magic that surrounds you in the everyday moments of your life. Through this energetic exchange with the Universe, you're welcoming in more opportunities for blessings to occur.

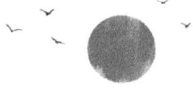

Give yourself permission to smile, to sing, to dance, to be happy. No one else can do that for you. Don't let others' experiences keep you from having your own. Your energy of joy uplifts the vibration for those around you.

Ask yourself with radical soul-honesty: Where are you denying yourself the joys of life's experiences? Where are you withholding aspects of your true authentic self? Where are you feeding into the chaos of the collective versus having faith in the divine order of creation? Where are you envisioning a new life but refusing to take actionable steps? Your miracles are awaiting your recognition.

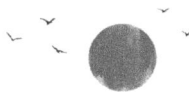

It's the soul's natural yearning to grow and evolve. You've seen where you're holding yourself back, and now it's time to begin your ascent into the next great adventure of your individual evolutionary history. Be brave and claim your personal power.

Difficult decisions might be necessary, particularly when it comes to taking action and overcoming fears. This will lead to a breakthrough and a sense of freedom within where you had been restricting yourself. Remember that you are the creator of your reality and the master of your emotions, your mind, and your own internal world. Connect to the pure essence of your eternal soul and allow for the expansion that's trying to come through. Your soul's truth is on the other side of your fear.

Pause and nurture yourself, particularly as energetic momentum is gaining and more physical action will be seen going forward. Finish any projects that are outstanding, address any conflicts that need resolution, or simply allow yourself to rest and replenish your spiritual energy. Don't lose your faith in what's still being created.

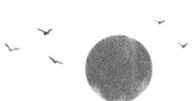

You're going to begin seeing the fruits of your labor with abundant manifestations coming to harvest. Although these might seem like miracles, you're being reminded these are just your own creations coming to life in the physical realm. You are more powerful in your own divinity than you can even imagine because you are connected directly to GodSource energy. As you come into yourself, you come into your power. As you come into your true, authentic power, you understand that your manifestations are a direct effect of what you hold within yourself because you are working side-by-side with the Universe.

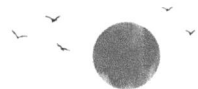

Whatever it is you're experiencing in the current moment, you're being called to have faith. Trust in yourself, trust in the situation, and trust in the Universe. Keep your vision clear when it comes to manifesting your dreams.

The past is the past. You experienced what you did for a reason, but every day is a new day and every moment is a chance to begin again. Start by forgiving yourself and others for the past pain, disappointments, and hurts. Let go of what was to embrace what is and encourage what will be. This redemption is your path forward.

You're coming out of the chrysalis and ready to spread your wings after your metamorphosis from caterpillar to butterfly. Now it's time to show the world who you are.

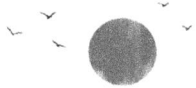

It's the darkness before the dawn. Your external world might seem scary, uncertain, or full of chaos, but don't feed into the fear. Take time to yourself or spend an hour outside—feel the sunshine on your skin, walk on the grass, touch a tree. Ground yourself. Embrace your family. Laugh. Nurture your inner child. Smile at a stranger across the street. Wave to a neighbor. Send love to each other. This is how you raise your vibration and change your life. This is how you begin to change the world. Where there is love, fear holds no power.

When you seek shelter from the storm within the higher heart, you remember there's nothing to fear. You are always connected, always loved, and always safe. You remember that the sun is still there, still shining, just temporarily hidden behind the clouds. Rest assured, these clouds will clear.

In remembering your divinity, you recognize that you are meant to thrive, not survive. In recognizing your sovereignty, you acknowledge that you no longer have to submit to the expectations of your own past self. In embracing your self-empowerment, you understand that you don't need to struggle in another's reality. You create your own.

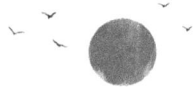

Use your emotions as your barometer for navigating your path. How are you experiencing certain situations? Do you feel energized and motivated or drained and depleted? This is your intuition telling you whether or not you're in alignment. Proceed down a different path or make new choices more in tune with your higher heart. Your soul's path will always be opened to you when you're aligned to love.

Instead of seeking for love in another, focus on the love that's already a part of your reality, that's already within you. Focus on your growth, your path, and the life that you're creating. Draw your energy back to your present state of being to fully engage in the love that exists in the here and now.

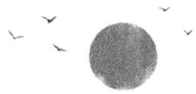

Romance is an energy of love that expresses itself through you. Bring more romance into your life by cherishing and honoring the love within yourself. Buy yourself some flowers, treat yourself to a special dinner, or write yourself a love note. Spend some time romancing yourself and invite the world to romance you back!

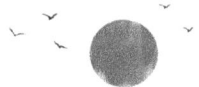

Let love grow. Release attachment to what you think love should be as you let go of the lack that hides within the subconscious caverns of yourself. You already have everything inside of you, including your connection to one and all. Let this love within yourself grow and watch how that love then expands within your world.

Love is all around you, woven through the tapestry of this world. It's in the sunlight glistening on leaves and birds flitting from branch to branch. Love is the natural course of energy that makes up the very foundation of the world. The more you begin to feel the connectedness of love within all things—and within yourself—the more you understand you're never lacking anything. Consciously choose love.

Hear the Universe when it speaks to your heart. Believe it when it whispers that you're worthy of this life and the people who love you. Listen closely when it reminds you that you are more than enough.

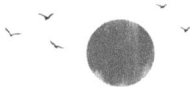

Love is never lacking. Love is never wasted. Bring your focus back to the love you have in your life now—your family, your friends, your animals, your passions, your work—and let it fill you up completely. Let it make you whole.

The Universe, in its infinitely loving nature, wants to bring you what you want! Meet the Universe halfway by trusting that when you take that leap of faith, those golden opportunities will be waiting for you on the other side.

You've been asking for a miracle, perhaps feeling frustrated by its lack of presence in your life. Miracles happen every day, in every moment, through a shift in energy and perspective. It's the mind's limited thinking that makes you believe in finite resources and solutions. Keep your heart open to every possibility. Your miracle is already here. Believe!

The seed has already been planted; now it's time to step back and let it bloom! Just as you would trust in the seed's own ability to grow, so, too, are you being asked to trust in the natural course of your life. All is occurring in perfect timing.

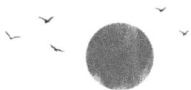

Continue to shine your light even when it feels hard, even when you want to give up, even when you can't see two steps ahead. You have a place in the world. You're here by divine design. The world may push against you, but you are loved for exactly who you are. Keep being beautifully you.

You might be feeling a little weary and exhausted by your journey. Take some time to nurture yourself and fill up your cup with love, compassion, and connection. You've fought the hardest battle there is: that of yourself. You've faced your shadows, your wounds, and your inner darkness. Through this ascension, you're finding your light.

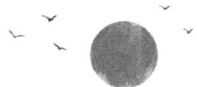

Don't be so hard on yourself! You're having a human experience while remembering how to be spirit again, and there will be times when your ego fights to survive and self-protect, forgetting that soul thrives within. You're clearing away the cobwebs, healing the past patterning, and breaking free from these illusions. Kindness and compassion for yourself is vital as you transform this thought patterning and shift your consciousness.

Take this time to rest. Spend some time in the silence of yourself and listen to the song of your own soul's guidance. It's almost time to begin something new.

Each morning the sun rises, and day always follows the night. This is the cyclical nature of the Universe and the evolution of your very soul. You may be going through a Dark Night of the Soul, or facing some other challenge or struggle that has you questioning your path, your experiences, or yourself. Remember: the strength and light that shines within you will never cease to exist.

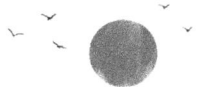

Energy is always flowing, and change is a constant as we continue to evolve. Whatever you're experiencing in this moment, know that it has the potential to create the breakthrough and transformation that your soul is calling for. Even if you can't see how everything aligns, have faith in the process and remain as present as possible in the energy of love. Sometimes, through the shadows of our experiences, we're asked to be the light.

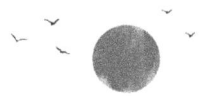

Your journey has already taken you so far… You're being asked now to step into the heartlight and go the distance. Don't hold yourself back from who you're meant to be.

You're being called to the next level of your life, which requires you to have the courage to dive deeper in connection to yourself. The more intimately you know yourself, the more lovingly you can connect with the world around you, which shifts everything both within and without. Through this leadership of yourself, you're having a profound impact on the world around you by energetically granting permission for others to do the same.

Quiet the overactive mind and outside influences through using discernment guided by your intuition. Bring the mind and the heart into balance by integrating your soul's wisdom. Keep walking the path of your heart.

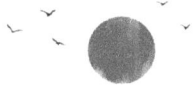

You're understanding that with every moment, you get to choose who you are and how you engage with the energies of the world around you. Your future is yours to create, and as you balance out within, your external world aligns to its highest potential. The seeds that you're planting now will bear their fruit come springtime.

There is unlimited potential within you, but where are you holding yourself back? Whether this is in a certain area of your life such as relationships and career or simply in your own growth and self-expression, you're being asked to look within and liberate yourself from outdated beliefs in order to expand as your soul is calling you. You've been playing it small long enough. Now it's time to set yourself free, break yourself open, and let your light shine. Now it's time to fly.

Commit to your journey and yourself. The more devoted you are to your soul growth and personal evolution, the more you're opening the door to your true self and the eternal wisdom contained within. Remember that you are an expression of the Universe itself.

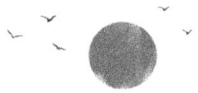

Your mission is first and foremost to be the truest and most authentic version of yourself you can be. Through exuding the love that is the core essence of all you are, you then embody that within your physical, human experience as part of your double mission. A world of infinite opportunity awaits once you tap into the highest-vibrational energy of all: *love*.

We're all interconnected, all part of the whole, and as such we're meant to be supporting each other. Where have you been blocking yourself from receiving love? Where have you been holding back from loving others? Take the time to identify with your needs and allow others to nurture you or be more nurturing to others.

Open your heart and see how understood you are, when darkness keeps you cloaked in the illusion of yourself. See how love can mend and heal and grow.

Let your open heart be the spark that ignites a revolution of love in your own life. Start by cleaning up your vibration and asking yourself where the old energy of self-criticism, resentment, fear, or other disabling energies are holding you back from fully connecting with and loving yourself? What learned cycle of internal self-thought can you change in the present moment, knowing you and only you have the power to change this within? How can you extend this grace and compassion to others in your life?

If you're finding yourself in need of encouragement and support, seek the courage within yourself to allow for this self-expression. If others in your life are in need of encouragement and support, allow yourself to be of service. Don't ever underestimate the power and value of a loving word or kind gesture.

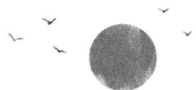

Love is meant to be experienced and shared, and when you feel the heart pull towards another, you're trusting in and following the wisdom of the infinite and all-knowing truth of your soul. Change the pattern of the ego mind—the place that holds onto fears, doubts, and old pains—and remember that love is safe. Go deep within your heart and listen to your intuition to fully understand and embrace this truth. Take a leap of faith by trusting in the Divine to support you and guide you. Let the Universe surprise you.

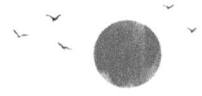

Trust the process. Trust that you are exactly where and when you need to be on your journey. You are right on time.

Be where you are. Remain present. Ground your energy. Remember that you're not who you were last year, yesterday, or a moment ago. This is the transition period as everything you've learned and understand consciously settles into your heart, your soul, the fiber of your being.

Your emotions are your soul's navigational system. Feel them, move through them, and release attachment to the story they're telling... But don't ignore or suppress them. Allow your emotions to rise through you by feeling their full force. They are your compass guiding you to what needs to be seen.

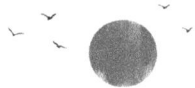

Episodes of anger, resentment, and other knee-jerk reactions are layers of old wounds being revisited for deeper healing and clearing. Can you recognize the pattern? Can you recognize the need for an alternate response? Step into your self-mastery and see where you can now choose compassion. Center yourself and focus on the love you feel. When you focus on the love and allow it to grow within your heartspace, any negative emotions and dense energy fade away. Love is the equalizer, neutralizing any negative emotion and raising your vibration.

The present moment is your point of creative power. Be mindful of the thoughts and stories you tell yourself. Shift your focus and watch everything around you begin to shift, too.

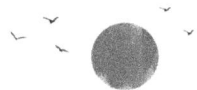

Take a moment to clear your mind of any fear and anxiety for the future. Shut off the news. Stop scrolling through social media. Just for a moment or two, step outside and feel the sunshine on your face. Close your eyes. Focus on the breeze. Listen to the birds. Breathe in and feel your heartbeat. Breathe out, imagining you're exhaling negative energy. Allow yourself to be present. If your mind chatters, focus again on the way the sun feels, the breeze, the birds, your breath. You shift the energy by shifting yourself.

Change your thoughts, change your life! When the heart and the mind come into alignment, inner peace is felt. This is where you become a master of the self. When you allow your heart and intuition to guide you and are mindful of your thoughts that like to question, doubt, and rage, you reach a level of surrender. That surrender allows life to flow seamlessly through you. In every moment, you have the power to change your thought patterns, to surrender the stormy sea within.

You may feel like you're in the eye of a storm, as if chaos is swirling around you, but this is a call to go within, clean up your vibration, and find your inner calm.

When we're born, we take on the energy of the world. As we grow up, we create beliefs based on the experiences we've had but from limited perspectives. Uncover what is real. What is your truth? What are your beliefs? When you know and love yourself, you have the ability to see the truth of yourself. What truth is or isn't serving you now? What is or isn't in alignment with your soul? What false beliefs were created that you can now rewrite to better serve your soul growth and best and highest potential?

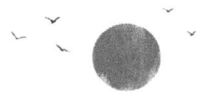

You're the artist holding the brush, the writer holding the pen, the musician playing the keys… You get to decide by your actions, reactions, and mindset the landscape your life is painting, the story your mind is writing, and the song your heart is singing.

It's time to recognize that you are on a sacred path and can change course at any given time. The Universe is always supporting and guiding you, and you're always exactly when and where you're meant to be. Even if you're out of soul alignment, there may be a lesson or experience to be understood before you're redirected. Trust the process and yourself. Be mindful of the unexpected visitors of old thoughts and patterns cropping up, tempting you to repeat old cycles. You're only as stuck as you feel.

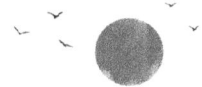

The dream that you keep close to your heart is taking shape. Your energetic alignment, through this heart awakening, is what's manifesting your dream into physical form. Tap into your inner strength when you feel discouraged and love yourself harder when you're experiencing lack. Hope always exists beneath the surface of heartache, so clear your energy and let that hope propel you forward when the opportunity presents itself.

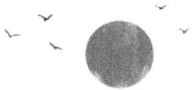

Be mindful of your thoughts pulling you into old patterns or beliefs. If life feels challenging, this is part of the release of the old energy. Listen to your heart and the wisdom contained therein as it guides you forward.

Remain grounded by going outside in nature or nurturing your physical body as you're called to. Finding a healthy balance between the spiritual world and your physical experience is required now as you move into a higher frequency and anchor into a new energy and version of yourself.

You've unlocked the doors of your own healing and are now stepping through the gate into the garden you've cultivated, nurtured, and bloomed within your own heart. Keep breaking generational patterns and traumas to create a life that is authentic to you.

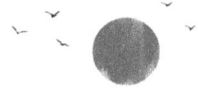

Your self-love is reflected in your self-empowerment. Connected deeply to yourself, you're no longer indecisive about who you are or how you wish to continue to grow and expand in that loving energy of personal embodiment and the higher-conscious frequency into which you've shifted. So much new is about to be experienced.

You are a powerful, divine being as part of the Universe itself, helping to expand not just within your individual life but in the very fabric of creation. Where have you been limiting yourself? Where are you settling for the stagnant, the mundane? Where are you not believing that you can create a life story that you love? Don't forget that you are human, too, and deserving of a fulfilling life.

There's a new energy of love that's stirring within the heart that is helping you to overcome your fears and making you want to take a leap of faith towards connection or reconnection. Playfulness and quality time together has the potential to build the bridge of friendship, leading you to higher levels of love with each other.

You are lovable, and you are loved. You are made in the image of GodSource itself, and so you are divine. As you become more accepting of this love for yourself, you'll be open to more love for and from others.

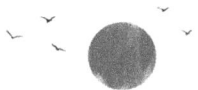

True intimacy exists within the shared heart-to-heart, soul-to-soul connection. When you see each other without masks or judgments, you're in pure acceptance and recognition of your divinity. Keep shining your light for each other.

Try not to judge others who might be judging you. Keep an open heart through your interactions and maintain that sense of peace within.

Love is a driving force for your life, as it's the very life-force within you. Are you recognizing this within yourself? You are not separate from anything in this Universe—from the moon and the stars, from the ants and the trees, from your loved ones or from GodSource. You're not separate from yourself. Connect to the love within and you connect to love in all.

Separation energy might have you and another perceiving the same experience differently, causing chaos and discord in your connection, but if you look from the soul's perspective, you're sharing one experience as two parts of the same whole. By approaching the situation or each other with fresh eyes in the energy of loving compassion and grounded empathy, you can help to clear the energy and ascend into a higher state of connection.

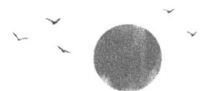

It's easy to look outside of yourself for validation and acceptance, but stand strong and stay true to yourself. Just because others may not understand you, it doesn't discredit who you are.

Life is a constant opportunity for expansion into more love. This expansion doesn't come from external focus but from internal reflection, evaluation, and growth. Let this gateway of opportunity heal the bonds of the past to see clearly the path your present state is creating.

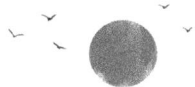

Look through the lens of love with every interaction with another to see the truth of the situation. Reflect on the experiences and see where collaboration and effective communication can bring balance to the relationship you're nurturing. Clear past cycles and allow yourself to be held in the container of love you share with each other. Through working together, you create a new and powerful cycle of harmony that has ripple effects through the Universe.

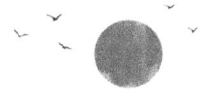

The door to your happiness is open, but are you willing to walk through it? You might have been trapped in the confines of your own mind, reliving a pattern of fear or trauma that seems to be holding you back from stepping into your true self and claiming your place in the world, in your life, or even within yourself. You have the ability to break free by shifting your energy. Healing is always available to you, inviting you to find your strength and move onto a higher path.

You have the power to transmute through the heartspace, through the power of love. Call upon your spirit team to purify anything that is not in alignment with the love of who you are and all that is. You are the open heart.

How are you reacting when faced with life's challenges? Do you let the obstacles affect you or do you rise to the occasion by shifting your mindset and energy within to allow the experience to become a catalyst for growth and learning? You, as a divine being, have the power to choose the direction that your experiences will take you.

You have a decision to either give into the fear of the ego or to hold onto the love within the heartspace. No matter what choice is made, know that this is creating an important transformation within yourself.

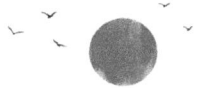

Difficult times show us where the wounds are so we can continue to open up to more love within ourselves. Keep breaking through the old patterns and beliefs by shifting your perception. Understand your shadows by turning your face to the sun. You're expanding in ways you never imagined. The actions that you take are the movement you create to bring more sunshine and joy into your life.

You've been experiencing a trial by fire—challenges and obstacles meant to test your self-mastery and the lessons you've learned on your journey thus far. Do you recognize yourself yet? Can you see that you are love? Are you aware of yourself as a divine being transcending lower consciousness? You might be reflecting on the older versions of yourself and the life you created within those past frequencies and feeling a sense of loss. Allow yourself this time to grieve and process who you were but don't forget to embrace the beauty of who you are and the magic of who you're becoming. These initiations have shown you the truth of the soul that resides within—beyond the illusions, beyond the pain templates, beyond the patterns and expectations and identity structures. It's time to step forward, share your magic, and embody the new soul-template of love.

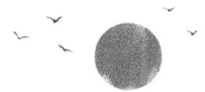

If you feel like you're being blocked by the Universe at every turn, take a moment to consider whether or not that's your soul's path or your ego's path. The path of your soul will flow easily, as the Universe conspires to lead you in the right direction.

Resistance is an energetic block that keeps you stuck in old programming and stagnant ways of living, unconsciously preventing you from stepping into your personal empowerment and sovereignty. Claim your highest potential through the energy of divine surrender as you allow yourself to ascend to a new level of consciousness.

Every thought, action, and choice in your life creates a ripple effect, extending farther than you can imagine.
Live with intention.

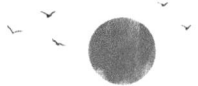

Your heartlight is guiding you along your path, leading you to the creation of a new life. Where there was struggle, there is now ease. Where there was pain, there is now joy. Where there was anger, there is now compassion. Where there was fear, there is now love. Your awareness and self-realization is the key to walking this path. Allow yourself to sit within the discomfort of change and among the shadows of transformation as you create magic for your life.

While you might be trying to figure out how it all pieces together within the limited means of the ego—perhaps even feeling trapped or stagnant in situations that feel out of your control—the Universe is reminding you that it is always supporting and guiding you. If you tune into your heartspace, you'll find that your soul has all the answers, guidance, and wisdom of the Universe itself. You're being asked to surrender in the trust and faith that this infinite wisdom is weaving the tapestry of your creation with you. Your deepest desires and prayers are always being answered.

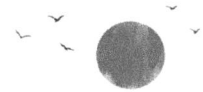

Your ability to manifest or co-create with the Universe comes first from your recognition and then from your embodiment of your sacredness—your connection to the Divine. You're dispelling the illusion of separation through believing in the expansive energy of the Universe and the power of love. As your heart continues to open through your spiritual and emotional development, you create a new life, a new way of being, and a new world. We all hold a piece to the puzzle of the collective creation. What seeds are you planting and nurturing?

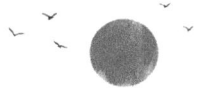

It starts with you.
With one spark you can ignite an entire revolution of love.

Go within and feel the whole of the Universe there. When did you stop having faith? When did you begin doubting? Return to that place of surrender and watch your miracles unfold and new blessings take place for all that you thought you lost.

You are and always have been unity. You are and always have been one with the Universe and one another. Tune into the sacred breath. Connect with your inner knowing. Be still and know that it's all within you.

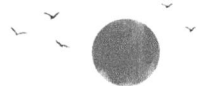

You're never abandoned and never alone. Whether this is friends or family or community, others are supporting and holding space for you in the energy of love so that you can heal until you are ready to hold that space of love for yourself. Be gentle and compassionate towards yourself as you renew your strength.

Your inner child wants to be seen and heard and is reaching out to be held. Take a moment to sit with your inner child without reaction or defensiveness. Hold that patience and tenderness in your heart as you speak soul-to-soul with the parts of yourself that want to be understood.

Keep your energy tuned to positive outcomes. Have faith
that all is well and trust that all will continue to be well.
Allow yourself some time to reflect and rest, and reach out
for support from others as you need to. You don't have to
carry so many burdens on your shoulders. You're not meant
to bear the weight of the world on your heart.

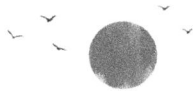

The more you appreciate the world around you, the more
your world will reflect that energy by appreciating you.

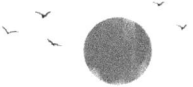

If you're feeling unappreciated, abandoned, or forgotten—
or in generally low spirits—know that you're not alone.
You're in a transition period where the old energy is still
releasing and with it, old emotions and beliefs might come
to the surface. Turn to your soul family for support. Shift
your focus from what's ending to what's being created and
to that which brings you joy. There is so much aligning
energetically that will reveal itself soon.

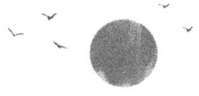

Where are you feeling depleted? Keep turning to
GodSource to replenish your energy. Have patience with
yourself and your journey.

It's time to move on from something that is no longer aligned to an old way of being, of loving, or of living that was dimming your light or not valuing you for the truth of who you are. This could be a relationship, a job, a location, or simply a state of being that you're releasing as you honor your self-worth. Spend some time in meditation and connection with yourself to listen to your heart and trust your intuition as you prepare to take your next steps of soul expansion.

Change is a constant in our lives, but the only thing holding us back from the changes we want to make is fear. Your ascension journey is helping you remember how to rise out of the comfort of the ego, which holds onto the familiar, in order to embrace the new with an understanding that you are safe to follow your soul's path.

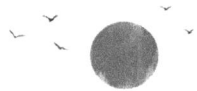

Within the human experience, we tend to hold onto old versions of ourselves when we're really meant to ascend beyond our perceived limitations and reach our highest potential. Don't listen to your own ego or the ego of others that try to hold you back from your own transformation. Courage is found within you.

Old relationships and situations might be falling away at this time, which can cause disappointment, grief, and heartache. Take some time to look at the bigger picture and see how the pieces of your life are aligning to move you into the next level of your journey, including welcoming in those who are on the same vibrational wavelength as part of your soul family.

Part of growth and transformation is being willing to identify and let go of the people, places, and things that are no longer in alignment with who you are on a soul level. This doesn't mean cutting those things out of your life completely, but rather allowing them to settle into the background as you raise your vibrations and step more fully into who you are. Who do you choose to be? What is still holding you back? Listen to the soul of yourself. You have every answer within you.

Love them freely... Let them grow away from you, let them choose another path, let them be what and who they need to be. Let them go. Their love for you isn't up to you. If they choose to love as you deserve to be loved, that's your blessing. But how you choose to love regardless? That's *your* gift. To love without conditions, to love without expectations. To love in your truthful expression and overcome suffering, to love in happiness and experience bliss. This is what you're here for.

Don't dim your love, but expand it. Love is already yours—
the Universe is ripe with it. Open the door to your heart
and receive love in the infinite ways it wants to enter.

Endings create new beginnings, and both can happen simul-
taneously. You have the awareness now to recognize change
within your life for the natural evolution that it is rather than
something to fear. Keep surrendering any resistance.

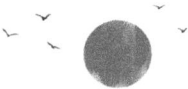

You've ended a major cycle of not only your evolutionary
journey but your life experience as well. All that was past is
coming to completion, and in this present moment you are
reborn to create your future. Be bold in your creations—
dream big and have the courage to take those steps towards
what fills your heart. Surrender the fear and resistance, and
trust in your own inner wisdom to guide you.

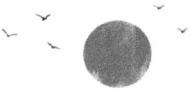

What do you need to let go of? What are you still holding
onto? Let go of the control, let go of the resistance. Let go
of anywhere you are not trusting. When you fully put your
faith in GodSource, that's when miracles occur
for success and abundance.

As you continue to evolve in consciousness, you might feel like you're caught between two worlds. In essence, you are, as there is the old third-dimensional matrix in which the planet is now transcending and a new dimension of higher consciousness that you're anchoring in. You are part of the bridge between these worlds as the planet continues its mass global awakening. Remember the tools you've acquired and the awareness you've reached on your journey. Continue to maintain your inner peace and open heart.

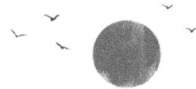

Feeling stuck is the egoic mind keeping you trapped in one of two ways: the comfort zone or survival mode. Both stem from the basis of fear, but this fear is an illusion keeping you from rising into who you truly are. Remember: you are a soul with the power of your life's creation within you.

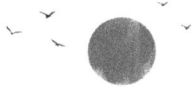

You get to choose your life. No one else can do that for you. Step into the heartspace, set down the pride and ego, and allow yourself to follow the flow of where the Universe—and your very soul—is trying to lead you.

It's time to level-up! Your entire world is about to transform from all the work you've been doing, so don't let fear or frustration disrupt your flow and knock you out of alignment. You have the tools to transcend old patterns and habits that kept you locked into old cycles. Don't stop your soul growth now!

This situation has the potential to break you open and change the direction of your life. However, this might mean a crumbling of the old foundation you had built. Let this experience break you through to something better, something that you never expected.

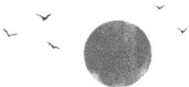

Everything is a matter of perspective. When you look at something within a limited frame of reference, you close your mind off to the broader perspective of what might actually be there. See things clearly by considering all angles. There are new perspectives that are trying to come into view.

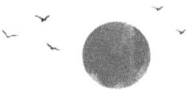

You're beginning to sing in tune with the song of your soul. Listen closely as you're guided back home to yourself.

The more you raise your vibrations and consciously shift your focus, coming more into alignment with yourself, the more the Universe arranges itself in order to bring you your manifestations along your best and highest timeline. The Universe wants to bring you everything you want, but it's up to you to be mindful of your vibrations and thought patterns by moving out of fear and into alignment with the greatest vibration of all: love.

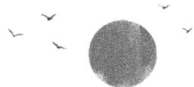

You're understanding yourself and your own power. As such, you're understanding the power of the Universe. You create together, with the Universe always aligning you with your best and highest potential based on your present energy. Life is always unfolding for your expansion, and you have the power to direct your own destiny.

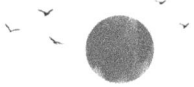

Be mindful with your actions! Rather than rushing in reck- lessly, merge the practical with the passion to create a sense of balance in order to enjoy more harmony and forward momentum for your situation.

You might experience resistance when it comes to forward movement, especially in the internal battle of the ego versus the intuition as past patterns make themselves known again. Awareness is your key to growth, for it's through your discernment of these patterns that you have the power to create conscious change.

Slow and steady clears the path. While you may have a desire to charge brazenly ahead, be grounded in your pursuits and listen to your inner knowing for guided action. This will help you release any blocks and clear the resistance for more success.

You're finding yourself questioning your path, your life, yourself, even the Universe, but remember that without the questions, you wouldn't have your answers. Connect to your inner knowing within the heartspace. GodSource is pure consciousness, and you are one with God.

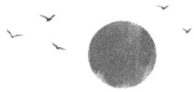

Your crisis of faith is a call to surrender, drawing you closer to GodSource and your inner self. This is a time to block out the noise and external influence and sit in the solitude of your own eternal wisdom. Allow yourself to receive in the highest octave of love. This is where your faith becomes stronger.

You know who you are. You know where you want to go and who you want to become. You know what it took for you to get to this point in your life journey—to become the person you are now—and what it's taking for you to keep going forward. You deserve to have faith in yourself.

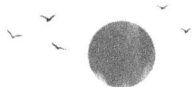

You are a unique thread in the tapestry of creation, with love embedded within every thread. Recognize love within yourself. Remember love is the thread that binds us all.

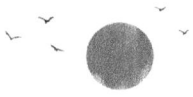

By constantly revisiting the past, you're continuing in old energy and creating from previous cycles. Allow for reflection in order to learn, but remember that your power to create your future comes from the present moment.

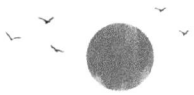

Nothing is forever, as change is always occurring. If life feels overwhelming or unstable, use the tools of your self-mastery—everything you've learned along your journey thus far—to bring yourself back to the present moment. It's here in the confidence of the present moment that you remember you're still creating whatever is to come.

Forward momentum is being established and change is occurring. If you feel like you're being pulled back into older versions of yourself or you're struggling to make changes, know that this is merely a chance for you to reflect and review before opening up to the new that's being created.

The smallest steps can yield the greatest results. Don't let the difficulties or challenges of life burn you out. You have an eternal spark within you. Fan the flame by finding joy in your life, in even the smallest measure. Those first steps can lead to a breakthrough for your life.

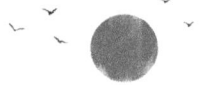

Bask in the joy of life! Call in your abundance and align with your manifestations through feelings of love and bliss. Leave the past behind you and step into the sunshine of this new phase of your life. This is your calling.

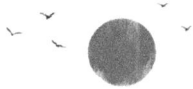

Every step of the way, in every single moment of your life, you're manifesting and making choices that bring to light your desires. The contrast showing you what you don't want is just as important as recognizing what you do want. You may not know exactly what you want or where you're headed, but your awareness is your superpower.

Ask yourself are your heart and thoughts aligned with the life you wish to lead? Magic comes in the moments you least expect because that's when the miracles occur—when you relax, when you let go, when you allow the flow of love to lead you. Are you finding the magic in every moment?

You are rising on the soul growth journey. The energy is lifting you into the higher heart as you become a master of your own energy and recognize the sacredness within you. Reflect on how far you've come in this internal transformation. Honor yourself here.

Are you ready for this new life? What you've experienced has led you here, and now this is your creation, the fruits of your labor coming to harvest. You've been cracked open to reveal the truth of yourself. From your rebirth, you're planting new seeds for your manifestations. Embrace this time. Embrace this new life.

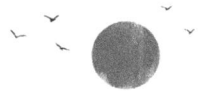

It's time to step into the light! You can stay in the background all your life, but you're meant to take center stage and claim the light that is you. Your soul wants to shine. Let yourself be seen.

You are who you believe yourself to be. Sit with the uncomfortable emotions as much as you can to see where those beliefs, mindsets, and perspectives about yourself stem from and allow yourself to release them without judgment by rewriting the script your mind may be telling you. Use positive affirmations to begin cultivating a new view of yourself in a more compassionate and loving energy.

Follow the threads of your heart. Go deep within yourself to discover the spark of your own life. Through listening to the song of your soul, you're experiencing the love that permeates throughout the whole of the Universe.

See the magic and divinity within yourself, and allow yourself to heal those places within that you deem unworthy or lacking in any way. You are a beautiful part of the fabric of creation. It's time you begin to believe how special you are.

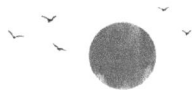

It's easy to question your purpose in the world, but you're already doing what you're meant to—living and loving. Be the best person you can be by growing, evolving, and embodying the energy of love. Your spiritual enlightenment is the byproduct of this embodiment.

As you continue to evolve and step into your true, authentic self, you're being called to express yourself in all of your divinity. This is the green light from the Universe letting you know you are ready to embrace your sovereignty, stand in your integrity, and share your truth.

You're ready to fly! You've been tested and tried, you've struggled and endured. But now that time of initiation is over. It's time to manifest the test of your strength and power. You've laid the foundation, and now you're being shown new heights. Your wings are ready. It's time for you to soar.

It doesn't have to be so complicated. You're serving the world simply by embodying the love that you naturally are. Let that love flow through you in your career, in your community, and in your everyday life. This is how you change the world. Let your actions be an expression of the love that you hold within yourself.

You're ending a tough cycle that has challenged you to grow, expand, and change within yourself and possibly even your physical world. You've been asked to look at your patterns, habits, and behaviors and see if they're in alignment to the highest version of who you are while you honestly ask yourself if through these physical expressions you're embodying who you *want* to be. Rather than trying to control this transformation, release the resistance to change and allow yourself to surrender this old energy. Connect deeply to yourself and the Universe to remember the essence of who you are: you are soul at the core.

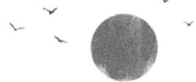

It's time to step into the spotlight of your own life, honor your sacredness, and live in your authenticity. Continue to express yourself from the soul. You are loved as you are.

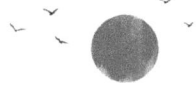

Step out from behind the old version of yourself and look at your journey with fresh eyes. There may be dueling perspectives or even an internal battle of the mind and heart, but shift to the higher lens of love in order to create balance and oneness within.

You're at a powerful point of transformation wherein you're being asked to find your internal strength and take action for your life, becoming the leader you always knew you were. This is healthy, conscious leadership in which you're invited to express your truth with clarity, direction, and a sense of purpose.

By bringing your shadows to your awareness, you're integrating all parts of yourself in the energy of love. The shadow isn't something to fear, avoid, or run from, but rather a fragmented and forgotten aspect of the self that is asking for more light. Through this self-awareness and acknowledgement of your shadows, you're connecting with yourself on the deepest level. It's here in this healing that you become whole.

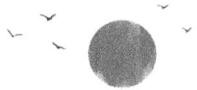

Make space for your own healing. Life is your greatest teacher, so accept responsibility for your life and invest in yourself. Hold yourself accountable for your growth and expansion, and that growth will reward you.

You're making love and peace a priority, releasing patterns of the past and old versions of yourself that no longer resonate with you. Don't hold onto that past version of yourself any longer. Feel the strength of your soul as your physical world begins to reflect this internal change in positive ways.

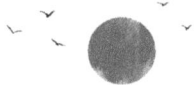

When you feel fully loved, anything seems possible. But when you allow others' judgments, expectations, or projections to seep in, it's easy to lose sight of your truth, which creates doubt and disconnection within. Remember that your connection to GodSource can never truly be lost. Create a self-love practice and return home to yourself.

Recognize yourself as your first true love, then explore that expression of love within your connections. Relationships are not only your greatest catalysts for growth, but they're a reflection of the frequency you're holding. Through loving yourself as you wish to be loved, you're becoming an energetic match to that higher frequency. This creates healthy and stable dynamics. Love yourself first!

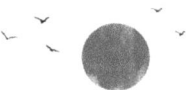

Love yourself. Be present with yourself. Enjoy each and every sacred moment. Plant your feet firmly on the ground. Play. Feel joy in your heart.

You've been your own worst enemy, but can you become your own best friend? Mistakes are experiences that create learning opportunities meant for growth. Forgive yourself for your past and stop being so hard on yourself when it comes to missteps that you may have made. It's time to treat yourself more kindly.

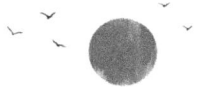

Commit to love as a whole and watch as love commits to you! Where are you still feeding the illusion of separation through disconnection from yourself and the Universe? Get to know your sacred self in the energy of love. When you commit to loving yourself fully, you're connecting more deeply to GodSource and the abundance of love that exists in the Universe.

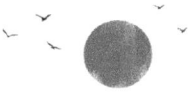

If you've been through heartbreak, look at your situation from a higher perspective to find the lessons and the blessings that you can carry forward. Recognize the capacity the heart has for healing, and keep your heart open.

While it may be easier to focus on the negative aspects of a person, situation, or experience in order to keep protecting the heart, part of your soul growth journey is the widening of your perspective to see beyond what is being shown directly in front of you. Consider all angles and look through a new lens—a lens of love, a lens of gratitude, a lens of compassion. You're being asked to not only believe in the power of love, but to *be* that power of love.

If love felt impossible in the past, it's now becoming available to you in healthy and conscious connections. There's a revelation occurring wherein whatever was making you question or doubt love is being cleared. Ask yourself what beliefs around love are you still holding onto? How can you show up for love in the way that you want love to show up for you?

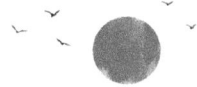

When the door feels closed, communication has shut down, or what is being portrayed in your physical experience isn't matching what you're receiving within your intuition, remember to connect back to your heart. Let it show you the way.

No matter what's being experienced in your physical reality, go within to find your peace. Your sanctuary is the sacred space within yourself where nothing can shake you. It's here that you know you're always supported, always connected, always guided, and always loved.

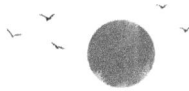

Remain kind, compassionate, and in your heart center. Use your intuitive mind to be aware of what may be happening beneath the surface of the physical experience. Ask yourself what's being projected or unspoken in your interactions with others. Speak your truth that's aligned with love. Don't let outside forces penetrate your peace. Love is not a weakness, and kindness counts.

Where do you still need to forgive yourself or others? How are you still blocking the natural flow of love by holding onto past pain and heartache? Be present. Let the past be in the past and don't carry that forward into your future. Forgive yourself, heal, and move on through this act of love.

Through forgiveness, you clear the past and open the heart to the flow of love that was previously blocked. It's here you are accepted without judgment, forgiven without blame, and seen as the divine soul you are. Begin to love yourself the same.

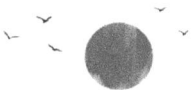

There's a strength that's found in vulnerability, for vulnerability is an expression of the open heart. You are your own authentic self, and no one can take that from you. This is your power. Don't be afraid of your vulnerability in expressing all that you are. Show the world the real you.

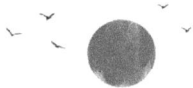

Your mission is an expression of yourself. The most important thing you can ever do is embody the highest version of yourself, in whatever way feels most natural to you. It's not about being perfect, but rather it's about embracing your divine humanity. Let love direct you so that everything you do becomes an expression of the love you are.

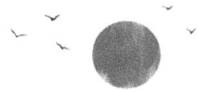

What are your emotions trying to tell you? Communicate with your emotions as you would communicate with a friend, for your emotions are a guide that lead you to a better understanding of yourself.

Your empathy is one of your greatest gifts, but empathy also requires boundaries. Allow yourself to extend your compassion to others with energetic, emotional, or physical support but be mindful of your own needs and output. Sometimes the best support you can offer others is holding space while they experience their own journey.

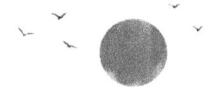

You're walking through the doorway towards your sacred destiny. Everything you've become in the process of the unbecoming has brought you here. Everything you've learned on this journey of soul expansion has led you to this convergence point of time and space. You're standing at the energetic entryway to the next level of your human experience through the evolution of your soul's journey home to itself. Here is where you embody your connection to GodSource. Here is where you recognize the eternal seed of life that has been planted in all. Here is where you find yourself in the wholeness of every lost and forgotten fragment of yourself. Here is where you find yourself in oneness.

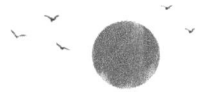

Move with the flow of the Universe, be present in the beauty of the journey, and follow your soul's guidance in the faith that your deepest desires will come true. Expect the unexpected along the way and trust in life to joyfully surprise you. Nothing is yet set in stone, as your story is still being written with every step you take.

This new start isn't just on its way, it's already here! Can you feel the gentle anticipation of it? Transformations are happening and new growth is blossoming. Keep faith in your heart, and keep your heart aligned to what it is you wish for this brand-new start. This is just the beginning.

The Universe is in constant motion. Even if you feel stuck, that stagnancy is only an illusion. Synchronicities are here to remind you that pieces are being aligned behind the scenes. Have a little more patience and faith while everything falls into place.

You're in the middle of a significant transformation wherein you're collapsing timelines of the old version of yourself and ascending into the new. It may feel uncomfortable during this transition stage as you release who you used to be and all you've come to know in association with that past version of self. As a result of this transformation, you may be experiencing external shifts in homes, relationships, and finances, or internal changes such as mindsets, beliefs, and perspectives. Remember that change doesn't have to have a negative connotation. Allow yourself to create a new future by embracing your growth and all the love contained within.

If you're experiencing a transformation or transition period, you're simply in the process of aligning to a new, higher energy. This phase might feel a little uncertain or even overwhelming, but have courage and remember the resources and tools you've learned along your journey to help guide you through.

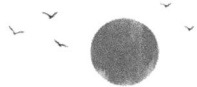

The part of you that's dying out is the old pain patterns and traumas of past experiences that kept you from recognizing your own divinity. The spark of the Universe is within you. Remember how special you are.

As your consciousness expands by allowing old patterns and beliefs to be released, you're understanding what love is—and isn't. Forgive yourself for times where you weren't able to recognize or give yourself that love in the past. Allow yourself to grow in love.

There's been a recurring pattern in your life created from a mindset or perspective that may have served you once, but that no longer is part of who you're in the process of becoming. This old way of thinking or viewing the world, a person, a situation, or even yourself may have been part of a trauma response—a survival or defense mechanism created during an unpleasant experience or time in your life that anchored in as a belief, and that belief has been replaying ever since. This spiral of thought has been holding you back and blocking you from expanding into a new version of yourself, keeping yourself caught in an endless cycle of repeating patterns in your life, relationships, and personal experiences. You may feel as if you're being blocked, but the Universe is always communicating new blessings to you. Take some time in reflection and see how are you receiving them?

You've been stuck in the darkness, but you're ready to step into the light. Lower the masks and let go of the illusion that anybody has authority, control, or sovereignty over you. Step forward into your personal empowerment and claim who you are. The world is waiting for you.

Your frequency and template of being is shifting as you transition out of old energy and embrace the journey of love. Give thanks for who you were and feel joy for who you've become and are becoming yet. The Universe is about to show you what happens when love expands and flows freely within you, as part of you.

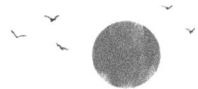

You're embracing a sense of home deeper within yourself or connecting to the feeling of home with another. Go within to find your truth and discover what home means to you. Your heart will lead you there.

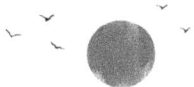

When you're honest with yourself about what's in your heart, then you can be honest in your connection with another. Intimacy is all about emotional connection that allows for a deepening bond, which creates true growth and soul expansion. Open your heart and let love expand with one another.

Whether you're reuniting or just meeting someone for the first time, this is a time of strengthening bonds and getting to know one another on a deeper level. Just as you have transformed, so are you now allowing your relationship to transform. Enjoy this time, enjoy this next phase of your partnership, and enjoy each other.

There is change on the horizon for your connection. You might be experiencing some external conflict resulting from inner conflict, but this is due to the ego fighting to maintain control while the soul wants to surrender. Past pain might be coming up to the surface for final clearing, including power struggles and resistance as the mind competes with the heart. Your soul is asking you to return to a place where love flows. Let trust in this spiritual connection reign over the ego's need for self-protection and preservation.

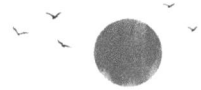

You're being asked to look at your external world and clear out your space, particularly being mindful of physical clutter. Your environment correlates to the health of your state of mind. As you cultivate your inner sanctuary, make sure you're tending to your outer sanctuary as well.

There's a storm whirling around you, but you're the calm at the center. Because of your growth and evolution, you're not affected by the chaos and conflict that surrounds you now. Stay in the middle, in the neutral center. Don't get sucked into the drama and toxicity that comes from a lower-vibrational energy. Ground yourself. Calm yourself. Remain in that place of peace within.

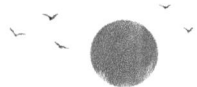

You're an anchor for the chaos around you through your grounding energy. By not taking part or elevating the chaos, you're naturally affecting the course of things to bring through more peace. Return to the calm within the chaos through your own self-awareness, compassion, and care.

Your mindset is the most powerful tool you have to create your outward reality. When you're in an energy of high vibration and prosperity, you naturally attract in high-vibrational experiences and material abundance. Similarly, if you're in lack or scarcity mindset, the Universe will respond in kind. Be aware of your thoughts and energy as you create your future.

From your present moment point of reference, you have the ability to shift your timeline to one that is more in alignment with your dreams and future visions. The path is always unfolding for you, being created by you.

No matter what the outcome of this situation is, you'll be okay. Feel the truth of this statement within your very soul. You'll be provided with support and solutions, but it's your job to release expectations and trust in the infinite wisdom of the Universe. Find your inner sanctuary in times of emotional unrest and be present with yourself as you allow for this surrender. The Universe has your back.

Have patience with your transformation and remember the caterpillar doesn't become the butterfly overnight. Hold space for yourself and others throughout this growth period. It may feel like you're experiencing a rebirth or starting over from scratch, but keep surrendering to your soul's path and trust in the divine unfolding as it reveals itself. You're never so lost that you cannot be found.

Spiritual maturity means having the emotional capacity to honor, recognize, and love yourself enough to take responsibility and accountability for your life and the role you're playing within your human experience. Release any shame or guilt for your past and resolve to make new choices from a conscious frame of mind.

Come into alignment with what lights you up and become a magnet for the Universe to bring more of that same passion into your life. You're moving out of the old template of survival mode and into an energy of thriving with a heart full of excitement for the life you're creating.

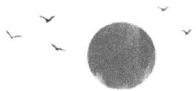

Loss or setbacks in your finances or material world may have led to difficult or even destructive paths. Remember who you are at the core instead of dictating your life based solely on external value. Let your inherent worth guide your life by following your heart.

You have the strength and inner authority to change your life in any moment, and new doorways are always open to you if you allow yourself to shift your perspective and walk through them. Bring yourself back to the present moment, for it's here that you create your future. Trust that tomorrow will be better.

You have the power to change your circumstances. It's not always easy, and it may require inner strength, but you have everything you need within you. This is where you stand up and live your truth. This is where you have the power to choose better.

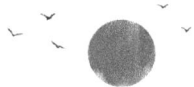

Take the leap of faith to step up and lead. Allow yourself to express yourself no matter how foolish you feel. You carry infinite wisdom within you. Allow yourself the opportunity to stand in your true nature and express yourself without fear.

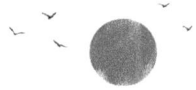

You may tend to silence yourself or allow yourself to be silenced by others, but your voice is meant to be heard. Find the courage within yourself to wake up to yourself, stand up for yourself, and express yourself as you desire to.

When you're true to yourself, you're standing in a place of
self-empowerment, which shifts the energy of your life.
You're beginning to integrate this understanding through a
new level of awareness, particularly in your view of the old
collective power structure. Power once meant control over
others, control over your environment, and control over
your circumstances. However, through your soul growth
journey, you've shifted to understand that this was all
illusion. Power comes from within oneself.

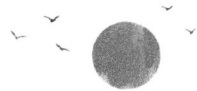

You are the Universe like the earth and stars themselves.
You're made of the same energy that made the moon and
the sun, the rivers and the trees. You are extraordinary. If
you're feeling lost in the illusion of lack and loneliness, take
a moment to remember where you came from.

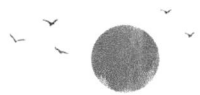

While there may be challenges or obstacles in your physical
environment, you're being reminded of your strength
and spiritual sovereignty on this evolutionary journey.
Continue to release subconscious fears and blocks, and
go with the flow in order to rise into your true nature as a
limitless being.

If you find yourself in need of nurturing, feel the warmth, compassion, and tenderness from the Divine Mother energy. Allow yourself to rest in her energetic embrace. Release all pain and past disappointments into her loving arms. You are safe, and you are held.

Your prayers are being heard by your spirit team, as they are and always have been here to support you with the loving energy of peace and spiritual nourishment. Allow yourself to receive this cosmic support and strength, and be sure to do your part by nourishing yourself. Find your joy, practice your peace, and hold the energy of love. You are here during this time and space, in this present moment, for a purpose. You belong. You are loved.

You are meant to be here, and you are so deeply loved. Don't give up. Don't for one single second think the world would be better off without you. You're shining a light in the darkness just by being the love and soul of who you are.

Break out of the consciousness trap by shifting the energy of your beliefs. This takes practice through changed behaviors and thought patterns, but the more you shift your perspective, the more you're able to change your belief and liberate yourself into a new life.

The lack of a physical manifestation within your life may be causing heartache and longing, but you're being reminded that there is more to the Universe than meets the eye, and you don't have this longing without purpose. What might seem delayed or failing to present itself is really just aligning for the best and highest potential. Remember: it's always better that you believed.

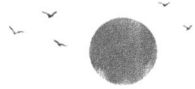

Your experience is leading to an awakening wherein you are learning to surrender and have faith in not only yourself but that to which you pray. You're beginning to understand that the divine unfolding of your journey is part of the gift. Keep going.

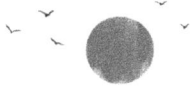

If you're feeling defeated, know that your strength is being renewed. Fuel that strength, ignite that courage, and be brave enough to take the first step towards making choices for your own creation. Change begins not externally but within you.

What once seemed like a distant or impossible dream is now becoming your reality through your transformation. Resistance and stubborn or prideful mindsets may have you holding onto old energy, which is causing you to doubt your dreams, but through surrender expansion occurs. Don't stop dreaming now, and don't hold yourself back from who you're becoming. Are you ready to see how far you can fly?

With every new cycle that begins, coming on the heels of another's ending, there's bound to be a little bit of fear, especially as you present yourself to the world. You're reminded to show off those wings—you've earned them!

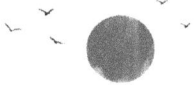

Don't be afraid to take that risk! You never know what's right around the corner when you gain that courage for your leap of faith. Take the first step forward and see where it leads.

What would you do if you knew you were safe, if you had complete trust in yourself and in the Universe? Ask yourself this question in honesty by going deep within. What would you dream? What risks would you take? What would you do? Take that guided step.

Your dreams are manifesting even in the present moment, so there's no need to worry. By remaining present and in a state of appreciation, you step more into alignment with yourself which then helps those dreams manifest.

You are exactly where and when you need to be. Now it's up to divine timing and the Universe for this to unfold. Take action as your heart moves you, but be open to receiving. Allow the Universe to surprise you with something big, something loving, something of which you're worthy.

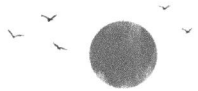

If you were to walk back through your life and be shown every trial and every triumph, every struggle and every success, everyone you've loved, everyone who's loved you, and every life you've affected just by your being in it, would you finally believe that you're worthy of this life?

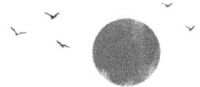

You may have been in an energy of lack, hiding away from the world in the caverns of the wounded self. But transformation is occurring, and you're about to undergo a beautiful metamorphosis. You are your own savior. You are your own light. You have the strength and courage within you to break through to the other side of this transformation. You have the power to change your life.

Faith stems from the heart. When you live in your faith, in the space between trust and acceptance, you begin to see with the heart, and what was once unseen can now be perceived through a higher lens.

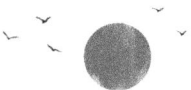

Abundance is a mindset that allows you to receive and feel gratitude for all that you have in your present life. Accept your current situation while holding the vision for what it is you're creating. Through your surrender, you're allowing the flow of energy that leads to change within your physical circumstances.

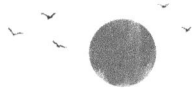

A new, stable foundation is being built in a relationship, but in order to have this new beginning, you have to leave the past behind. Allow the past to remain in the past as you embark on this adventure in a relationship that is more grounded, secure, and committed. Now, you're moving towards something greater together.

There's a call for intimacy and conscious connecting with regards to the relationships in your life. Your heart is longing to reunite and reconcile with a member of your soul family. Set your differences aside and refocus your attention on what unites you, for what unites you is simply love.

You're joining with another in a union of hearts through a love that has endured. As you enter the next phase of a connection, remember that partnership requires support, reciprocity, and healthy communication for commitment. Together, you stand stronger.

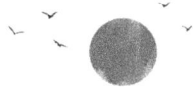

Happiness has always been yours as an innate part of you, but the inner power struggle of your mind versus your heart led to resistance which blocked your way. Through your surrender, you're coming into a balance of self, creating new ways of being, experiencing, and living. Forgive yourself for the past. This is your breakthrough to a new and unfolding way.

Your mind and imagination are powerful tools for creation, but action is required. Lean into the fiery element within you and be bold and brave with your intuitively-guided steps. A new cycle is opening up for you.

It's time to move towards something that opens you to more love and uplifts you in the highest light, enabling you to see your truth, your value, and the love within in a beautifully expanded way. This could be a relationship that you're spiritually connected to or soul work that you're passionate about. Connecting with your higher heart will reveal clarity for your path and grant you the courage to take that initial step forward.

More clarity is entering your life. Where before things may have felt difficult—obstacle after obstacle with no end in sight—you're understanding that this was all orchestrated to help you level up and bring clarity to yourself, waking up a part of yourself that might have still been stagnant. Soon those gray skies will be bright and vibrant with color.

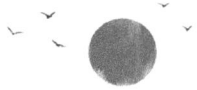

A decision is being weighed and energies are being balanced. Anything that was out of harmony in your life is now being brought to justice as you find balance within yourself.

You may be finding yourself in need of guidance, but you already have all you need within you. It's time to trust your own intuition and your connection to the Divine itself. Ask for support and support will be given. Let the Universe work through the world around you to receive the answers you're seeking.

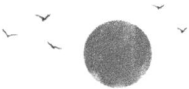

Remove your faith in all that is outside of yourself and have faith in what's within, for that's how you manifest. What you believe is true inside of yourself is what you will see in your external world. To transform your external world, you must transform yourself.

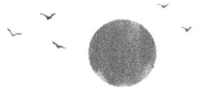

You're beginning to feel more confident and empowered to take action towards your dreams. You've anchored this next level of consciousness into your heart where all of spiritual life resides. As you're shifting with these energies, your physical world transforms. Have patience.

Your dreams need nurturing in order for them to grow. Seeds aren't just planted, they have to be watered, given light, and nourished. You've been planting seeds for a new dream, wish, or goal, but now it's time to put in the work to allow for them to bloom. You've got this.

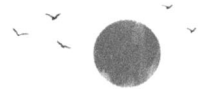

You may have been seeing signs and synchronicities relating to a specific manifestation, even reminding you about your dream or desire if it's something you'd forgotten or it felt too out of reach. You're being asked now to release the energy of the old version of yourself who had once held that desire—not because the dream or the desire isn't worthy of you but because the new energy is what's going to bring it to physical form. The old version of yourself had the vision. The new version of yourself is what aligns to it in your physical experience. Expand your consciousness and release any old limiting ideas or beliefs. Remember the infinite and magical nature of the Universe. It's this energy that is a part of you, this space from which you're manifesting. Keep following the compass of your soul as your dreams take root.

You may have a few different options being presented to you wherein you're considering which path is best. This is causing some confusion, perhaps even some pressure, as you intuitively know you want the path that feels happiest. But what is your happiness? What creates that wish fulfillment? Connect with yourself on an intimate level and tune into the innocent nature of your soul, the part of you that knows you best.

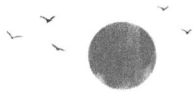

The path of least resistance is the one most aligned to your soul. Reflect on the opportunities available and see which feels peaceful and at ease. Don't be afraid of making a wrong decision as you can always course-correct, but allow yourself time to consider all options and what they mean to you as you create your path forward.

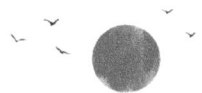

While you may feel weary at times, know that the light is always within you. Rest, but don't give up. Surrender doesn't mean defeat.

If you're being called to take a break or step back, know that this is simply a temporary pause for you to step into your intuition and power. You're currently going through a leveling-up, shifting into love consciousness. As a result, you're being called to tap into your intuition and connection to the Universe to get your bearings and affirm you're in alignment with where you want to go.

You're shedding layers of old energy quickly and manifesting new beginnings at rapid speed. Allow yourself to slow down and enjoy the journey, as it's all part of the process.

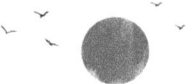

As you step more fully into the soul of yourself, recognizing your power and divinity, you're realizing that this is who you have always been beneath the third-dimensional, human construct. There has been a breakthrough as of late wherein you're recognizing and remembering the power within yourself and who you are on a soul level.

Take that leap of faith! The doorway is open, but it's up to you to make the choice to step through it in order for the Universe to bring your heart's desires to you. Unblock the heart and step out of the energy of self-sabotage. Trust that the Universe is always supporting you.

Feel brave enough to express yourself with healthy boundaries and communication. When you stand in your authenticity and no longer hide behind illusions, past conditioning, and old paradigms, you're staying true to yourself. Be strong and confident enough to speak this truth.

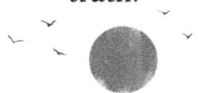

There's freedom in your self-expression. Acknowledging and speaking your truth creates a lightness within yourself, as it prevents the energy from being suppressed and festering within. Experience the power of your truth moving through you as you speak the words out loud, even if only to yourself. Liberate yourself from the attachment to those words and their experience. Feel their hold over you dissolving until they become nothing. Set your soul free.

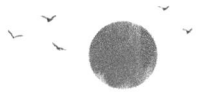

Embrace your story—the one you lived, the one you survived, the one you fought for, the one in which you thrived. You hold your story in your hands, and this is your power. Your story is your evolution.

Where are you holding yourself back from sharing your story? You may have felt out of control through your past lived experiences, but your power comes from claiming your story as part of your evolution. Your story has the ability to heal both yourself and others experiencing similar journeys, and it's here that you write your future.

You have to feel your feelings in order to release them. Allow yourself to be radically honest with yourself about how you're feeling. By bringing your emotions to your awareness, you're no longer letting them control you. Once you can acknowledge your emotions, you're able to consciously shift the energy to create a more positive outcome.

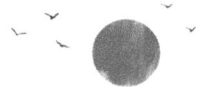

To heal doesn't mean you're broken. To heal means to remember your wholeness, your divinity, that you were never anything less than love in the first place.

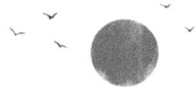

As you heal yourself, you help to heal the planet and all that is a part of the whole. As you heal through love, you become love. Strip away the layers of who you thought you were and step into your true authentic being. You are love embodied.

You are not just your body. You are not just your physical world. You are a soul of magnificent energy experiencing the world within physical form. Appreciate your external world and love your physical body as you remember to honor the fullness of the creation that is you.

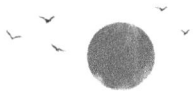

Liberation is experienced within the self as self-determination, willpower, and personal sovereignty. This is your very soul longing to be heard. You are never powerless and never helpless. Call upon your inner strength to release yourself from anywhere you don't feel free. Listen to its call and follow its guidance to lead you.

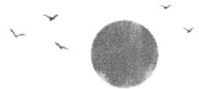

A new era for your spiritual evolution is here. The past cycle has been the catalyst for your soul's growth—a leveling up in your spiritual understanding and self-mastery. If you've been feeling stuck in a period of limbo, rest assured this is changing. This pause was laying the foundation and putting the pieces into alignment for the forward momentum of your manifestations and goals.

You've been put through the fire, clearing those old layers of your life as you've been reborn. This is your homecoming. Welcome home to yourself.

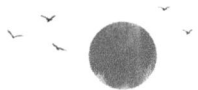

Turn the page. Close that book. It led you to where you needed to go but not to where you're headed now. It's placed within your heart so you can carry it always, but now it's time to start fresh. This is a new you. This is your new story. How are you going to write it?

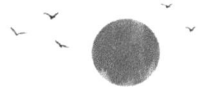

Light doesn't have a goal for which dark corners it wants to reach. It just shines and allows itself to be. So be. Shine brightly. Love fully.

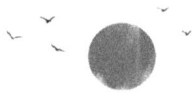

You make a difference in the world just by being in it.

WANT MORE MESSAGES?

Subscribe on YouTube for the original Daily Energy Draws,
Soul Path Readings, Sacred Channelings, and more!

Susan Dawn Spiritual Connections
&
Susan Dawn Ascension Connections

FOR YOUR JOURNEY

From healing resources to inclusive learning tools, continue
your soul growth journey by exploring all of the services
and products at Susan Dawn Spiritual Connections!

Ascension Connections
Healing & Harmony Activation Series
Tarot in Translation Series
Courses & Programs
Meditations
Spiritual Guides & Journals
Tarot & Oracle Decks

ABOUT SUSAN DAWN

Susan Dawn is a spiritual coach and intuitive energy practitioner at Susan Dawn Spiritual Connections, LLC with a focus on soul connections and the ascension journey. Intuitive by nature and deeply connected to the universal energies around us, Susan works directly with GodSource to bring through messages of love, support, and learning as well as healing activations for the soul's expansion.

Connect with Susan on social media at @susandawnspiritual!

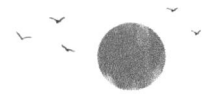

ABOUT SUSAN DAWN SPIRITUAL CONNECTIONS

Susan Dawn Spiritual Connections is a sacred space for your soul growth journey and the home of Angel Aura Energy Healing! Bridging spiritual understanding with real, human application, Susan Dawn Spiritual Connections helps you nurture your own self-empowerment while encouraging connection to your magic and divinity.

Learn more at www.susandawnspiritual.com

ACKNOWLEDGEMENTS

WANTING TO CRAFT THESE MESSAGES into a digestible format has been an overwhelming but worthwhile labor of love. Thank you to everyone who made this book possible!

To Ruth and Renee, a mega-dose of gratitude for helping to transcribe hundreds of daily channelings. Thank you for your support in tackling such a huge project!

To my family and soul sisters and brothers, thank you for your unconditional love and encouragement along my own journey. Your belief in me is so deeply appreciated and a thousand times returned.

To the Susan Dawn Spiritual Connections community, thank you for your open hearts. I am endlessly grateful for your support and am honored to be a part of your journey. Thank you for being a part of my own path as we walk each other home.

www.ingramcontent.com/pod-product-compliance
Lightning Source LLC
Chambersburg PA
CBHW051633120626
46551CB00014B/2055